# My garden of flowers and broken pieces

*by Nika Erčulj*

FOR

*you and I.*

For the parts we have played,
and the parts we have yet to play.

Dearest,

I began writing this book about five years ago. When I wrote the
first few words, I remember feeling so lost and confused. I was bat-
tling my mental health issues and often felt like I was engulfed by a
tornado that wouldn't stop spinning. My world felt cold and lonely,
and there were so many gloomy days.
I couldn't see myself or my future in any shade other than black.
I didn't know if it would ever stop, and I definitely didn't see a way
out, but I decided to give it a try anyway.

This book reflects the journey I embarked on in the most honest
and vulnerable way. From feeling like I was spinning out of control
and not seeing any signs of light, to looking up at the stars with
hope and a newfound love for myself.

I would have laughed if you told me my grand adventure would
have taken me back to myself. At the time, that would've felt
disappointing, or even silly, but now I know that in the depths of
my heart, I found everything I was ever looking for.

To say I'm nervous about letting you into my ocean of vulnerability
is an understatement, but I've gotten to know this fear quite well
over the past few years, and now I know it must be worth it.

I hope that through my words, you uncover pieces of yourself and
send a few more drops of compassion and love to those parts that
feel lost or unloved. I hope that by the last page, you too, get to see
yourself with new pieces of understanding and acceptance.

*I love you. Thank you.*
*Nika*

PARTS:

1. No sun

2. Searching for the moon

3. Dancing with the stars

# PART 1
*no sun*

# TRAPPED

I don't like this place. It's cold and dark and it feels like a constant wind of suffocation. I'm sitting in a large birdcage. The cold wind is circling around me and, weirdly, I've gotten pretty used to it by now. The cool breeze touching my skin feels almost soothing. I've been trapped in here for a long time. Even though it's a dark and lonely place, it's my home. I have no idea when I became used to it and I wish I knew how I felt before all of this became so weirdly comfortable.

I remember being a little kid, trapped in this sad, so-called home with one small toy. I didn't really mind. I wasn't happy, but I was okay. I was always okay. I pretended that this cage was a happy place. It's weird because I started believing myself. I created a whole new world in there. I became friends with the cage.

I never allowed myself to feel sad and the thought of me being trapped in this horrible place was so frightening that I just wanted to stay as far away from it as I could. I somehow always knew I'm going to escape and live like I'm supposed to, but then - the worst thing happened. The wind stopped and the cage was suddenly unlocked. I could now open the door. I feel paralyzed and weak. I hate this place, I hate that I still call it my home. I hate how dark, cold and lonely it is. I hate looking outside and seeing a beautiful sunny sky and people laughing and hugging. I hate it because I know I could feel the same way.

It's terrifying because it feels like this cage has been an excuse for such a long time, and now - it's gone. The doors are open, but I feel too scared to leave.

DANCING

I was blindly spinning in never-ending circles
trying to find something light and warm

It was a cold and lonely dance
but it was the only one
I knew the steps to

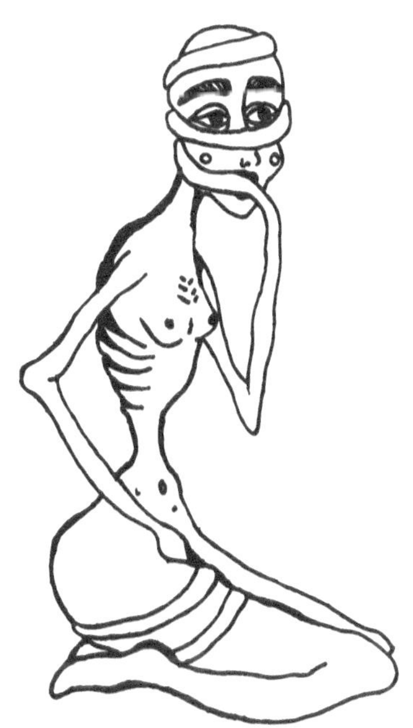

# NOVEMBER

It was a cold and sad November, like every year. I got reminded of things I wish I could bury and I revisited emotions I thought I left behind a long time ago. I was freezing walking around the city and I saw trees letting go, just like I should have years ago.

Everything just felt cold. And then I bumped into you. I don't know how or why, but without even thinking, I let you in. I let you see the depths of my soul and you warmed me up.

We counted the stars together and danced under the moonlight. You held me tight and for the first time in my life, I felt safe. Safe from the world, but most importantly, from myself.

Your hug was nothing compared to all the other ones. It was the only thing that made me fall away from my thoughts and let myself just be. I felt like I was breathing and melting into you. It seemed like not even our skin separated us anymore. I was scared, of course, but my love for you seemed like a flower finally opening up to the sun, and with every touch and every word, I drifted further away from my biggest fear - love.

The whole world just turned light pink, and I ended up surrounded by warmth and dreamy gaze. My bones turned into branches full of white, pretty flowers, my cheeks were no longer pale, and my touch felt softer than ever.

It all looked like a dream, and I was paralyzed by the thought that it could all be just that.

Fear crushed me down to my knees and suddenly, I woke up to a cold December.

# LOVE LOST

There are things I'd rather not say,
but my mind can't escape the way my heart beats.

It can't forget the things you said aloud,
the words that tainted your angel-kissed lips forever.

It can't forget the way you looked at me.
The way you punished me with coldness
and poisoned me with unsureness.

Your cold, tainted words felt like a robbery,
and what was stolen shows no sign of reappearing.

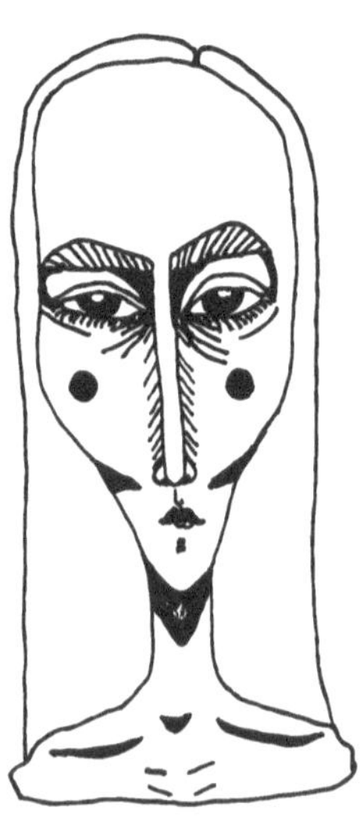

# (IN)SANE

Today I noticed how heavy and stiff my body feels, as she ever so gently kisses my cheek, after greeting me with those hungry, yet familiar eyes.

When she opens her mouth to speak, my body starts to ache and cry for help.

I'm mindfully creating a sword, as her words attack every sane part of my complicated thoughts and touch even the brightest of smiles, buried deep down in my heart.

She can seem like a beautiful flower, but she's more like a knife, slowly cutting me into the person she so desperately wishes me to be.

After she clears her mind, lets out her unbearable emotions and cleanses her aura, she leaves my body clenched down in the corner of a pitch-black room. Her words cut so deep into my existence, I no longer know what's mine and what's hers. I am left with a burden she no longer wants to carry and I feel more lost and alone than ever.

But don't worry, maybe next time she'll replace her knife with the brightest smile and it'll all be okay again.

# THE WAVES AND THE STORM

He dismissed me like I was an old, forgotten painting that's been resting on his wall for years.

He went on with his day and left me hurting. No words, no kisses, no affection - a not so unusual routine for the two of us.

There haven't been any signs of love in this household for years, and every once in a while, my thoughts sweep me up from sweet dreams and take me to nightmares and fears full of "it's all because of you".

# THE SHATTERED GLASS

I spend my days and nights looking at the garden right in front of me. When I close my eyes and fall into a deep daydream, I can remember exactly how it felt like when my tiny feet touched the freshly cut grass.

I spent every day here. Picking and planting, laughing and running from one place to the other, carelessly and freely.

Now I notice the beauty of the garden doesn't feel the same. It's filled with flowers, some dead, some barely standing upright, and others overpowered with a strength that feels almost evil.

Under the plants lay pieces of shattered glass, shimmering in the April sun. There's a part of me that wants to just go in, destroy everything and start fresh, but the other part wishes to gather the strength to dive deep into the soil, the roots, and heal even the smallest corner.

But it's too frightening.

How many times will a tear blur my vision, as I say goodbye to the ones no longer with us?

How many times will I collapse in disappointment as the broken ones, no longer want to stand up straight?

How many pieces of glass will I find buried in my skin, and how many times will I scream?

I just want to know if this garden was ever really pure, or was it all just my childlike imagination? It can't possibly go from a beautiful piano tune, sunshine so bright and warm it almost feels like it's leaning on your shoulder... to this, a complete chaos of disappointment, sadness, and anger.

Most importantly, is it even mine, and if so, am I a flower or a shard?

These are the words
that cloud my
already frazzled mind,
as my brand new
journal soaks the
tears fallen from
my sleepy eyes.

# NO WORDS



A forced smile, my muscles tight and heart numb.

The whole world froze,
while my brain resided to complete chaos.

I could feel my insides weeping, burning, sobbing.

I had so much to say
but no words to give.

# DAYDREAM

I was woken by birds and a calm breeze again today. I opened my eyes to find a light of sunshine sitting on my hand. It reminded me of you. I smiled and slowly closed my eyes again, just so I could see you.

You greeted me with a loving hug and a laugh more beautiful than any song I've ever heard. You took me to your favorite place again and we laid down in a field of flowers. You told me about your day and I told you about mine. We picked flowers, talked for hours, explored the depths of our souls and just laughed all day long. You seemed so happy and full of life.

The night came and as the sounds of the animals nearby started to turn quiet, so did we. While you were admiring a distant shining star, I was looking at the one right in front of me.
Your eyes were lit up by the moonlight. They looked so innocent and so pure, yet so sad at the same time. I could see the bruises and scars left on your body and I wanted to stay by your side, hold you forever and make it all okay again.

I wanted to protect you from the world, but you never allowed me close enough, and so here I am, revisiting you in my daydreams, wishing you could pull me close and let me love you.

# UNCOVER



Maybe one day
I'll bump into you
and let you know
what love without fear
*is like.*

# I CAN'T LOVE YOU

I was so scared of your love, although it was all I ever craved.

The love you poured into my heart was the only thing keeping me warm that winter.

Your hug felt like ten thousand blankets all wrapped around me and when you looked at me with those pretty eyes, I swear all the hurts of the world dissipated.

I would spend the days we were apart daydreaming about your soft-spoken words and thoughts that were so beautiful I could imagine wildflowers growing from them. I couldn't bear the thought of hurting you again, so I ran.

I pushed you as far away from me as I could and pretended I never knew how to love you.

# CRUMBLES

It aches and it bleeds under those murky floors.

It longs to pour its tears of debilitating pain and uncover the scars and broken bones left by those who could only see the blackness of a starry night sky.

At times it clears those floors by smashing and screaming.

Not to debilitate or destroy,
but to free.

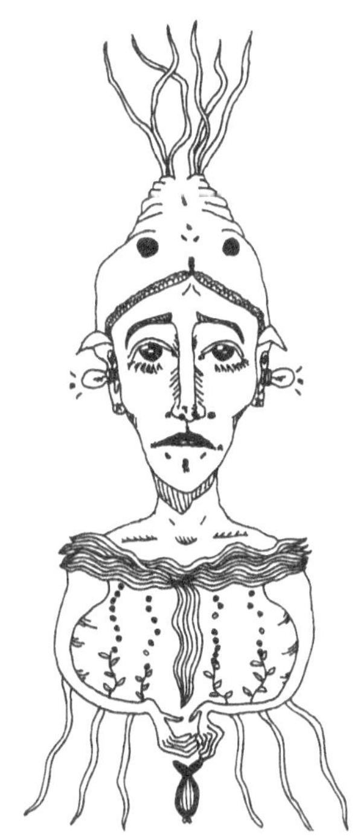

# HOW HEARTS BREAK



Is my heart broken
because it's been loved before,
or because it's never truly been?

# RAGING ECHO

I woke up trapped in the feeling of people raging inside my head again.

I'm laying down in a pool of freezing water losing the ability to move. My hands and feet are tied up with a string of thoughts.

The nearly pitch-black cave is quieter than ever and there are people running from one side to the other, walking over me, as if my body had dissolved into the water I'm laying in.

I'm trying to teach myself to scream, but the fear inside my head won't let me. My hands feel like heavy stones and my soft touch has turned into a painful scratch for help. My back is collapsing in on itself and I'm crying invisible tears of pain. I'm tied down, but I keep on trying to run into the unknown, while that one line echoes almost like a melody.

I'm waiting for time to pass, but seconds are turning into weeks, and when the sun finally rises, I hide. I am blinded by the light, though it's the savior of my drug.

# A DIFFERENT KIND OF LOVE

The love you gave me was not like the one that kissed my cheek
and swept me into darkness I haven't been able to escape from.

Now I fear that no amount of I love yous, hugs and kisses could ever
heal the fear and void residing in the deepest parts of my bones.

# SAVIOUR

I'm so lost
and the sad part is
I'm waiting for someone to save me,
because I no longer believe
I can do it myself.

# HIDE AND SEEK

Isn't it strange how the whole city reminds me of you?
I come here every once in a while, in hopes of maybe running into you
again. I imagine how you would greet me and what you would say.

The songs we used to listen to play in my head as I walk down the
lonely streets and desperately search for you. Instead of my steps,
the city sunset or tall old buildings, all I can see are our memories.
They've been haunting me at night and have now joined the daytime.

All these memories of your words, your kisses and hugs are like
drugs I can't leave behind. I can see your features hidden in other
people's faces. When someone touches me, I desperately wish I
could replace them with you and I swear I hear your voice in the
quiet. I can still feel your hand touching my body, your lips pressed
against mine and your fingers tangled in my messy hair. Your smile
is my favorite, but the thought of it now only makes me cry.

Without you here, I feel so small and I find myself walking down
the same streets trying to find you. But I've come to know that a
game of hide and seek can't be fun if I'm the only one playing.

# PART 2
*searching for the moon*

# WHEN RIVERS TOLD STORIES

I sat on a rock next to him. Will was in his sixties. He was slim, tall and sported a long grey beard and round Harry Potter type of glasses. I watched him collecting rocks, organizing them from the lightest to the heaviest and then throwing them into the near river one by one. There was this confidence about him. As if he's seen wars, lived through unimaginable adventures and met the most extraordinary people, yet wasn't fazed by any of it. Like none of it ever mattered. Accompanying the odd, somewhat contradicting confidence, was his vast emptiness. It oozed out of his life and sort of fit in with him like ashes after a burning fire. You could see it in his eyes and if you'd observe long enough, you could find glimpses of it in his laughter. When I sat next to him, I often felt like he was miles and miles away. As if an important, essential part of him had already drifted far away and there was no string strong enough to ever pull it back to him.

Still throwing rocks he so neatly organized, he began to recite stories from his past. Will was a somewhat mysterious man, so this rare occasion excited me more than most things in my mundane life. His stories felt like the movies he invited me to watch months ago. They were filled with the deepest, darkest human emotions that usually stuck with me for weeks, like a gloomy fog resting above overcrowded cities. The stories I was fortunate enough to hear would've shaken up the toughest souls and maybe even leave some eyes teary tod red. But to me, nothing was as sad as watching someone you admire slowly give up. Like life was being pulled out of them and now they're drowning in gloomy oceans full of sadness and defeat they can't escape from even if they tried. I know Will gave up trying a long time ago and I go through internal battles trying not to resent him for it. On crowded streets where most would see people laughing and bursting with life, he saw loneliness and desperation, so vast and so thick he often got lost in it. In his words: it only reminded him of how pointless life had become.

That day we spent by the river - not so surprisingly, it was when he showed the most vitality in months - I asked him what in his life had he lost. He never told me anything personal and avoided most questions about the people who I thought he once loved. At first, he laughed as if I recited a scripted joke from one of the papers he loved to mock. Then he took a long pause and stared into the river. I watched his eyes, anticipating an elaborate, grand story. But all I heard was, *"I've never lost anything, as I've never truly loved. Maybe if I did, I wouldn't have to wander this world, confused about how I got it all so wrong."* He sighed, shrugged his shoulders and, lacking any emotion, added *"I suppose I should've paid more attention to the cheesy quotes telling me to not fear that which I love."* He concluded with a laugh and that was it. That night, I biked back home with a heavy rock on my chest. Although his story was brief and most of it was recited in a somewhat cynical, joking manner, it hit a part of me I always felt lingered somewhere deep inside.

RELAPSE

You're the drug of my misery.

You fill me with such emptiness
it echoes for miles away.

You feed the monster within me
I so carefully locked away.

You remind me of the worst darkness there is
and maybe that's why you feel so good
*...because you feel like home.*

# MY GARDEN OF FLOWERS AND BROKEN PIECES

I'm sitting on my kitchen floor on some gloomy Wednesday, feeling like I haven't slept in about two weeks. There's a puddle of tears around me and I'm trying to find my broken pieces again.

I've experienced heartbreaks before, many kinds, but I always knew my heart will be filled with flowers I planted, like it once was. But this feels different. This feels like you stripped my garden of breathtaking flowers and turned it into a desert. A garden of sand. There's something so empty about it. Lacking life and pure love. And now, I feel like one. So cold at night it makes me shiver and unbearable during long, hot days.

I don't know how long it'll take me to replace the sand and plant beautiful sunflowers again, but right now, I'm trying to decide whether I even have the strength to leave the broken pieces sitting on my cold kitchen floor.

Every time I try to pick one up from the growing puddle of my tears and join it back with the rest, I tremble with this inexplicable shiver. A shiver with something so evil and impure about it.

These pieces aren't mine. They don't make up a beautiful blue ocean, a field of flowers and words that make you feel like everything is going to be okay again. I feel like placing them back together would twirl and suck me into this tornado of unimaginable sadness.

So maybe I should stop searching for something that isn't mine and never has been, and instead, start writing my own story. The one where I am the one completely in charge. The one where I can be exactly who I've always wanted to be. The one where I get to decide who I let in and who I leave out. The one where I can do everything

I've ever wanted. The one where I get to feel everything I've ever felt, no matter how dark or intense it is. And the one where I get to make everything around me beautiful again. The one where I get to fill my mind with stunning art and live in my own little gallery by the ocean.

Maybe you broke my pieces and stripped my garden. But maybe, just maybe, this is all I've ever needed, and maybe I finally freed myself.

# FALLING IN, FALLING OUT



How can two people
shape each other
and grow apart
all *at the same time?*

# REFLECTIONS

In the depths of my closet lays a picture. Familiar eyes staring back at me, reflected on the shiny paper.

I grab the photo and sit down on my messy bedroom floor. I close my eyes and drift away, just to visit her. She greets me with an innocent smile, secretly covering sadness, grief and rage. I try to ask some questions to unravel the tension, but she just passively stares back at me with fear anchored somewhere deep inside her. After long minutes of silence, I see tears flooding down her rosy cheeks. She tries to quickly wipe them away, but they're like waterfalls refusing to stop the flow.

I see the immense pain take over every inch of her body and I am paralyzed. I froze in seconds and no matter how much I try to move my limbs and reach for hers, I can't. Somewhere in the distance, a familiar voice keeps repeating nasty words I've heard all too many times. It goes on and on for minutes that feel like years. As my new T-shirt soaked up my tears, I opened my eyes to a debilitating discovery — my own reflection.

# REFLECTIONS

In the depths of my closet lays a picture. Familiar eyes staring back at me, reflected on the shiny paper.

I grab the photo and sit down on my messy bedroom floor. I close my eyes and drift far away, just to visit her. She greets me with an innocent smile, secretly covering sadness, grief, and rage. I try to ask some questions to unravel the tension, but she just passively stares back at me with fear anchored somewhere deep inside her. After long minutes of silence, I see tears flooding down her rosy cheeks. She tries to quickly wipe them away, but they're like waterfalls refusing to shut the flow.

I see the immense pain take over every inch of her body and I am paralyzed. I froze in seconds and no matter how much I try to move my limbs and reach for hers, I can't.

Somewhere in the distance, a familiar voice keeps repeating nasty words I've heard all too many times. It goes on and on for minutes that feel like years.

As my new T-shirt soaked up my tears, I opened my eyes to a debilitating discovery - *my own reflection.*

# LITTLE MAN

Little man, I was once in your shoes in the middle of this windy storm, trying to understand which way the wind blows and decide whether to let myself go or to learn how to dance with it.

Little man, I've walked in your shoes before and I remember how strong the storm can get. It sometimes feels like you'll get torn apart and like every shelter you build gets blown away.

Little man, I was once in your shoes and I was trying to fit in them again, so I could take your little hand and create a shelter that would keep us away.

But I am here sitting in a cold, dark, crowded room with my hands shaking and my eyes watering, terrified because your shoes don't fit me anymore.

I guess, little man, I was trying so hard to teach you the steps that I failed to realize this is my dance, not yours.

So you, little man, you'll soon learn your own steps and after a few more tornadoes we'll dance this storm away.

# HEARTS BREAK LIKE GLASS

Your coldness still hurts me to my bones
and I feel your betrayal lingering
in parts of my body that feel the heaviest.

Many years ago you were my first heartbreak,
yet the after-effects can still be felt
with different faces but warmer hearts.

# FLOODS OF HEARTBREAK

I want to know what pure, passionate love feels like.
I want to know if someone I love
could ever love me back just as much.

I'm scared I'll have to shed parts of myself.
I'm scared I'll have to numb my pain.
I'm scared I'll feel ashamed of the hurt, that's hanging on
to me, like dark eyebags resting on my face after I've just
pulled an all-nighter.

Will I always have to beg to be seen? To be felt?
I fear I'll unleash my love for someone who will tear it apart,
like I've done many times before.

I'm tired of confusing monsters for loved ones.
I'm tired of my disappointments stacking on like floors that make
up skyscrapers in cold, *lonely cities.*

# ROSE GARDEN



Her love seemed like a rose garden.
Beautiful from the outside,
but incredibly painful
once she finally *let you in.*

# SHE WAS AN ENIGMA, THE MYSTERY OF MY LIFE

I often referred to her as ice on fire. If that's a definition one can use, a part of it felt true, although still uncomfortably confusing.

Her mystery felt like the deepest parts of an unexplored ocean floor. There was a whiff of darkness, yet purity. It felt oddly familiar. As if there were pieces of me I couldn't dare to uncover while hiding in her. Safe to say I could never wrap my head around everything she was. I think that's what made her special. There was no box to put her in, no words ever came close to describing her mind and even her eyes didn't give much away. But in some empty, quiet moments, you could feel how deeply human she was. How wholeheartedly she loved, even those who never understood the totality of who she was.

Most of us like to place pieces into boxes, but she was never one of those people. I think the vast emptiness made her feel at home, or maybe deep down, she longed for a definition that didn't defy all conventions. To be honest, I'm not quite sure. Throughout all these years, I was never able to see her through. To me, that's what made her so deeply, mysteriously, intriguingly beautiful. She was the enigma of my life. To this day, a mystery that remains unsolved.

UNTITLED


She is full of flowers
and broken pieces
that tell stories
most of us
are too afraid
to face.

I DON'T LET MY LOVE GROW

I'm trying to learn how to let my love grow, but I keep drowning in an ocean full of memories I can't escape.

I guess I always thought love would be easy. I thought it would be easy to let someone close enough so they could hold you, so they could love you. But when you hold me too close, my scars ache and I feel an overwhelming shiver of pain I could never explain.

It seems like I placed myself in a box and ~~tore~~ parts ~~that feel you thought~~ of me that feel most human and I keep trying to run through glass windows, but they never seem to break.

# I DON'T LET MY LOVE GROW

I'm trying to learn how to let my love grow, but I keep drowning in an ocean full of memories I can't escape.

I guess I always thought love would be easy. I thought it would be easy to let someone close enough so they could hold you, so they could love you. But when you hold me too close, my scars ache and I feel an overwhelming shiver of pain I could never explain.

It seems like I placed myself in a box and froze the parts of me that feel most human and I keep trying to run through glasswindows, but *they never seem to break.*

## TIME MACHINE

It felt very odd. It was like running into a loved one I haven't seen or spoken to in years and I didn't know what to think or how to act. You could sense the distance that grew between us through the years and I felt like I was walking through a field of needles trying to avoid getting hurt again.

Deep down I know this girl and how she feels all too well. Those feelings still linger in my heart and every once in a while, she visits me in my dreams. I know that we're the same, but all that fear and pain separated us years ago. I think I needed to leave her behind so I could get through pieces of heartache she wasn't old enough for.

I'm now ready to tie her shoes, take her little hand and let her walk beside me. I'm ready to get to know her and be the person she always dreamt of having by her side. I'm ready to do all this and more, as I know that every wild, free soul must be nurtured and loved in order to spread their wings.

# WILL YOU STAY, OR WILL YOU GO

Our lives have pushed us in opposite directions, far from where
we can touch or even scream to be heard.

When we finally come together again, we're like strangers
pretending we haven't just spent a lifetime together.
Like we haven't just shared the depths of our souls
and the secret, buried parts of our hearts.

I thought you, out of everyone
*… I thought you'd stay.*

# LOVE?

I am trying so hard
to get love from people
who have none to give.

Love?
They are *ice cold.*

The sun hasn't shined on them in years
and I don't even know if their hearts are still beating.

Love?
That's something they are deeply starved of

and love,
sadly they can only take.

# THAT SPECIAL SOMEONE

My heart feels like a labyrinth,
my mind like an unsolved puzzle
and I'm still waiting for someone new
who'd dare to solve it.

# COMMON MELODY

I'm playing a constant game of losing myself and then
finding myself again.

An exhausting battle of contrast, I can't seem to win.

In the midst of my chaos, I sometimes uncover pieces of
inspiration. I don't know how to explain, but I find it thrilling…
*being found again.*

The rush of discovery.
The unknown possibility.
The new.
The better.

In a way, it seems like I have spent months playing an exhausting
yet exhilarating game of hide and seek.
Who will I uncover this time?
*I never know.*

I find myself more and more suspicious as doubt clouds my
tangled thoughts.

What if what I keep uncovering are just pieces of me that have
always been there, but I've somehow buried at sea?

*Who knows…*
My mind plays tricks on me
and overthinking is the common melody
I know that contrast resides in me
and I might have to believe it's all heavenly.

# ANOTHER SHOT AT LOVE

Maybe we'll find long lost places that feel like home,
maybe we won't.

Maybe we'll find people whose hearts fill those places, or ours
would have to sing solo for a little longer.

Maybe our adventures will take us closer to who we've always
known we could be, or maybe they'll drive us even further away.

That's the beauty of exploring.
*It's the unknown.*
The hope that we might finally find what we've
always been longing for.

Regardless, my love, it's always, without a doubt,
worth another shot.

# FANTASIES

One day I'll swim with beautiful creatures and drown my thoughts in pure crystal waters.

I'll gaze at the stars, dance into the night and feel at home.

I'll fall asleep with clouds covering my body and wake up with the sun kissing my cheek, while the melody of my joy plays louder than the echo of my heartbreaks.

One day my body will no longer be covered in scars, but in beautiful colors of the Earth, and I will sing the words of the happiest of songs.

Until then, I'll get caught in a few more thorny branches of pain, I'll close my eyes for a few more days, wander far away and get *lost in my wildest fantasies.*

# WILD ANIMAL

With tears blurring my sight, I started to take down the art, remove the flowers and see it for what it's always been.

I can't describe the loneliness and sadness that took over me, as I stood there with my past staring right into my eyes.

I started to slowly break down the walls. It started with scratches, then went off pounding which led to full destruction of what once was.

I knocked down everything I've fought so hard to keep. I destroyed everything I once thought I wanted.

There was sadness, of course, but it felt right. It felt like someone finally opened the cage of a wild animal and *set me free.*

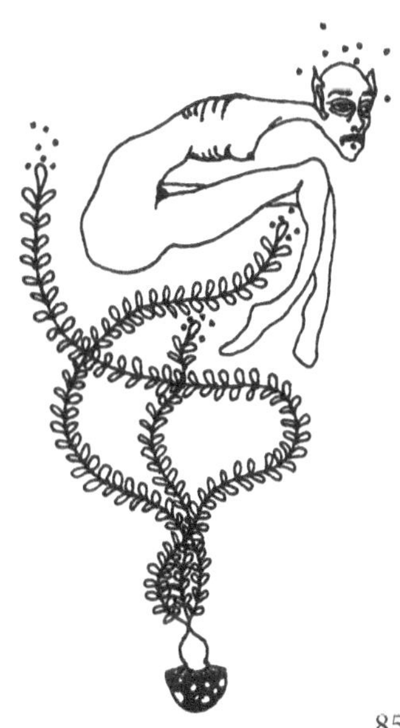

# PLAYHOUSE

Through the years, that little girl I used to play with
became a woman.

A strong and beautiful one, with a mind more powerful than a
storm and a heart bigger than the universe.

She still nods and listens. At times scared of who she might cross
paths with. At times even scared of herself.

But she's finding her way now.

I see it in her eyes, in the way she carries herself and the way she
smiles walking down the street. You can sense the wisdom of her
scars. They hold the type of power the sun does over the Earth.

# HOPE DIES LAST

I'll lay here for a little longer.

I'll rest and I'll heal,
but that's not where my story ends.

I have faith that the shadow
I've been living in for so long
can't exist
*without the light.*

# PART 3
*full like the moon*

# DISCOVERIES

Uncovering parts of ourselves
to sense the love and magic
that has always been there,
quietly and patiently waiting
for us to rediscover it.

*- The truth of who we really are*

OVERFLOWING



And now I rise with the wind,
my love is like a stream
overflowing from within.
It flows like a wave,
touching every stone, every bone, even the skin.
And if you ever return,
I will let you in.
But I will never stop the wind.

# NEW BEGINNING

I left everything I knew to
find everything that's true.

With heavy baggage on my
shoulders i've ~~accumulated~~
accumulated throughout the
years, exploring worlds i've
never seen before.

I traded my routine for freedom,
my shelter for my body
and my reality for a dream.

I hope I get lost in the best way
possible.
I hope I grow and change.
I hope I find meaningful
connections.
I hope I find what's hurting, take its
hand and find its blinding light
in the dull darkness of pain.

And lastly ... I hope I find my truth.
Regardless of what that
might be.

NEW BEGINNING

I left everything I know to find everything that's true.

With heavy baggage on my shoulders
I've accumulated throughout the years,
exploring worlds I've never seen before.

I traded my routine for freedom,
my shelter for my body
and my reality for a dream.

I hope I get lost in the best way possible.
I hope I grow and change.
I hope I find meaningful connections.
I hope I find what's hurting, take its hand
and find its blinding light in the dull darkness of pain.

And lastly... I hope I find my truth.
Regardless of what that might be.

# LETTER

I am in every corner of your soul, daydreaming about kissing your cheek and waiting for you to dive in and feel my magic.

I'm sitting here next to you whispering everything you've always wanted to hear, just wishing you'd see me and let me hold you in my arms until the fear and fog dissipate.

I am trying to show you the truth. I am trying to uncover your inner power, so you could see your true potential and that everything you've ever wanted belongs to you.

I am trying to show you who you really are, what you really deserve and let you rediscover what has always been there...
The simple fact that you are already whole, you are and have always been more than good enough and you are so very loved.

What are you still waiting for? Come feel the magic.
Don't worry, I'll show you the way.

*- Yours always, Self Love*

# WRITTEN IN SOLITUDE

My cure lays in the written word.

Here I find peace.

Here I find solitude covered by floods of understanding.

Here quietly lays my soul, shining through a warm, bright light, waiting for me to tune in and rediscover its everlasting beauty.

NEW WORLDS

From the very first time I saw you I knew you were something incredible and something I haven't yet experienced. You were filled with universes of wonder.

You showed me what it's like to remain deeply open when the world demands you to close. You showed me the beauty of my shadows and the tenderness of the scars I still carry.

With you, I explored new worlds and discovered a sense of freedom I had never felt before. I laughed to the point my stomach grew forests, and cried as though my cheeks desperately craved rainfall.

We jumped headfirst into a yet unexplored wild sea, and what we found still brings roses to my cheeks and ties knots within the depths of my heart I have yet to untangle.

I am writing this today, as I want to thank you. Through our adventures and wild explorations, I uncovered a part of me that was long lost and so badly wanted to be found.

And above all, I thank you for letting me love what is real and what is raw. I will never forget you.

# WISHES TURN TO PARADISE

I am planting flowers in my soul.

I am watching them grow into beauty and grace,
exuding the purest kind of love.

I am spreading it all throughout my being, watching it cure every
dying and forgotten flower, with soil so nurturing it only spreads
love, understanding, and magic.

The sun is shining so bright I can finally see the beauty of my
hidden shadows. And the water so clear and pure, with powerful
waves splashing away the thoughts that have been planted
long ago when there was only darkness.

I am watching this home slowly turn into the paradise I've always
desired. The kind where all is accepted and all is loved.

The dream I so patiently held in my hands as a little girl,
just wishing one day it would come true.

# OCEAN BREEZE

I am sitting on the edge of a cliff looking down at the waves of the ocean, taking in the warmth of the sun and the Earth.

I breathe in and I imagine my breath healing every cell in my body. As I breathe out, I feel a small tear running down my cheek and my hands naturally fall onto my chest.

I close my eyes and I breathe in again, now even deeper than before. As the fresh air fills my lungs and touches the most delicate flower in my being, I get a sense of overwhelming calm.

I belong here and this is where I feel safe. It's out in the open, in the shell that is my body and the wavering yet calm ocean that is my mind.

PICTURES

As I was going through every single picture in our old family
album, the time stopped and flew by all at once,
and I was filled with a mix of emotions.

I felt like I was slipping through memories and I remembered
every single one as clear as day.

I remembered my school plays, my birthday parties with my then
friends... now strangers. I remembered the dance performances
I now no longer know the steps to. I remembered how the sun
shined through the blinds of my old bedroom and how loving my
aunt was, although I no longer know
what it feels like to be held in her arms.

I've remembered people I would have otherwise forgotten and
memories that would have just remained passing seconds.

As the years went on, I started creating my own memories.
Memories I wish to hold close to my heart forever.

Every emotion, person and place so breathtakingly wrapped up in
beautiful nostalgia and every moment as something to remember.

# ALLOWING

The sun eventually always rises and all is awake bathing in its glory.

But do you ever fear our brightest star won't rise?
Do you fear the darkness returning, or do you allow it to
exude its magnificent power, teaching you the mysterious and
transformational lessons of the moon and the stars?

Do you ever doubt the sun's ability to come at the right time?
When you have taken in the
lessons of the starry night sky?

city of love

A few days ago I took myself on
a trip to Paris. I didn't come
here to find love, just to let go
of it. I came here to let go of
past wounds, forget about certain
words and special kinds of losses.
It's all been burning in my brain
for months on end and I wanted
to get away to finally leave it
all behind.

I shed.          I cried.    I healed.

I finally did what tears do
every fall - I let go.

I opened myself up to strangers
who became friends. I found
freedom in my steps, beauty in
my words and lust for my life.

I felt love for myself. The purest
type of love my heart has always
called me towards.

I guess Paris really is the city of
love after all.

# CITY OF LOVE

A few days ago I took myself on a trip to Paris.
I didn't come here to find love, but to let go of it.
I came here to let go of past wounds, forget about certain words
and special kinds of kisses.
It's all been burning in my brain for months on end and I wanted to
get away to finally leave it all behind.

I shed
I cried
I healed.

I finally did what leaves do every fall.
*I let go.*

I opened myself up to strangers who became friends. I found
freedom in my steps, beauty in my words and lust for my life.

I felt love for myself. The purest type of love my heart has always
called me towards.

I guess Paris really is the city of love after all.

# MY PATH



Oftentimes it's not simple.
It's often much easier to follow the crowd
and live a life others understand,
but I am not here to experience that.

I'm here for the magic.
I was made to chat with the sun, cuddle with the moon
and dance with the stars.

That's the path I will choose again and again.
A path where my heart can't help but sing and dance
*to the rhythm of my soul.*

# INNER POWER

My power might not have come with instructions,
but it sure came with a potential
for a revolution.

# JUST ONE OF THE REASON WHY I LOVE YOU

I know the past may have been dark and gloomy. You felt small, trapped and alone when the world around you was crumbling into pieces. I know how lonely and scary it must have been.

But I can only hope you find a true reflection when you look into that mirror resting on your bathroom wall.

I hope you see you've built roots more powerful than the oldest tree and notice the beam of light sitting on your shoulder, hugging you and kissing your cheeks.

I hope you see what I see when I look at you. I hope you see how you stand taller than the wisest mountain, with your head tilted high into the sky, while remaining so gentle and so beautifully soft.

I know it is hard to remain open when everyone orders you to close, but that, my love, is your biggest strength. Through all the losses and heartaches you haven't lost your humanness. You haven't forgotten what is real and true - that which is peacefully resting under the passing heaviness you so often feel in your chest.

# I CHOOSE ME

I choose to no longer ask for permission,
but instead, give notice.
*I choose to rise up.*
I choose to show up for my dream
and in a world that expects me to whisper,
I choose to howl.

FORGIVENESS


My love, why do you fear forgiving yourself?

As if the ocean of disapproval will take you down and
never spit you out.

You've so blindly adopted this unsettling truth. The truth that you
are innately wrong and need to censor your every move.

I see those parts of yours you so eagerly place in hidden corners.
I see you're afraid to share them with the world. I see you hide
them under your pillows at night and hope to
forget them by the morning.

But my love, these parts are the ones that will set you free and
uncover your sacred magic.

So climb to the highest mountain,
sing your innate song of love
and watch as the world heals.

GROUNDBREAKER

She dared to be inconvenient and she dared to be strange.

When something felt like it carried heavy weights of injustice, she unapologetically spoke of it from the tops of mountains and got even louder when they thought she was crazy.

She always spoke her truth, no matter who listened, unafraid of judgment and misunderstanding.

Strange, confusing looks only invited a big grand smile to her otherwise unamused, dull face, as she carried knowledge most didn't...

She knew the world can't possibly understand something it hasn't yet seen.

# BLOOD MOON LIGHT

Last night I sat on a rock near the ocean and spoke to the moon.

She was sharing her wisdom and uncovering my truth,
while the ocean lovingly held my hand.

I felt like they were carrying me and loving me in all of my
dark, dusty parts and shining their love and light on places
that haven't seen any in years.

They gently placed me back together again
and like the sweetest lover,
they held me through it all.

# HERE TO STAY

The love I have for myself is the type of love I used to seek out,
chase and never really get the hold of.

Now it peacefully rests in my body and it can never run or hide.
I don't have to hold on to it,
while my hands bleed and my eyes water.

This time it's different.
*This time it's here to stay.*

# FINDING MY WAY

I guess life is about finding what you believe in and what you'd rather leave behind.

It's discovering hidden, far away places that make you feel at home, and the people who fill those up.

Things you want to fight for and fight against.

It's falling in and out of every kind of love.

It's learning what peace is and exploring the freedom in the depths of wild waves and unremorseful storms.

It's randomly meeting people, not knowing how they'll change your life.

It's those spontaneous, late nights where everything so naturally, yet wildly falls into place.

It's about adventuring through young love not knowing whether it'll break you or softly place your pieces back together again, and in believing you'll be okay either way.

It's talking about your passions with your face lit up like a forgotten lightbulb and carefully searching for it in those you come across.

And most of all, it's finding purpose in whatever you come across.

Some say that's where you find *"the one"*, but I hope that's where *I find myself.*

# THE POWER OF A WOMAN

I am convinced there is nothing more beautiful
than a woman coming into her own.

Blooming like a gorgeous flower and uncovering her inner fire.

Stepping into her love, so strong and so full it overflows like a
flood, healing every heart and every drought.

## CHERISH

In my chapters of growth
I place my hands on my chest
I look to the moon and the stars for guidance
and I slowly place one foot in front of the other.

Silently I know these are the days I pick flowers
I have never seen before.

I bring them back home and smile as the garden
I'm growing blossoms and expands carrying
new lessons but mostly a lot of love.

# SECRETS OF THE HEART

And finally,
she cracked her shell,
as her mind
could
no
longer
contain the sweet
secrets of her heart.

# LOVER

I will put my hand on your heart to make you feel alive again.
I will catch your tears and help you wipe them away.
I will listen to your soft words and the silence too.
I will take your sadness and bathe it in my love.
I will take your hand and guide you to the light.

And lover, above all else,
I will always stand beside you,
cheering for your every step.

# MORE THAN JUST A WORD

*"Home"*
such a simple word.

A person or a box on the 99th street,
or maybe holding a child's hand,
a gentle hug between lovers,
a walk through the woods,
the second floor of an old building,
or a dip in the ocean.

Such a simple word, so many definitions.

I wish I could speak to everyone and ask about their shelter.
I wonder if any would say "my bones"
or if it'd be something like joy or freedom,
a sensation, like fuzziness in their stomach.

Such a simple word, yet so much emotion.

I know for many, home may have been tainted by people
whose hearts couldn't see theirs.
And to those whose home never knew any shade of love,
I hope my question doesn't blur your vision or make your
chest bleed.

I hope it nudges you to wander, create and choose again and
again until you find a shelter that will always keep you safe.

*I love the word home.*
Seemingly a box to some, but much more meaningful to most.
Universally undefined to just one simple thing.
To me, it reminds me of transformation.

Of a girl whose home never felt like one, so she went on to search for her own.

A quest for love and for freedom.

A creation of her own sanctuary.

# ONE LOVE



We now hold our hands together
looking toward different skies
for answers we have somehow forgotten
rest inside us all.

# DEEPLY FULL

And after all I found love.

*I found it*
in the depths of my heart,
the roots of my sadness,
in the hidden parts of you,
and in the beauty of the deep sea.

# ANCIENT

Life sometimes throws unexpected twists and turns.
Mysterious curves bending us in ways we never saw coming.
Reawakened memories.
*Unresolved hurts.*
Familiar, yet ancient.
Familiar, yet unbearably uncomfortable.

In times like these, I've found the most peaceful sound to be the
sound of my breath and the gentle beating of my heart.

Familiar, yet ancient.

Reminding me of the simplicity that lingers in the now.

*Alive. Blessed. Awake.*

In these moments, I stumble back upon the ancient truth of
who I am. I lift the heavy veil of chaos and collect the wisdom of
simply existing.

# THE PATH



Though the obstacles are heavy,
the past covered in gloom,
and there are still struggles in many corners,
I know it is all worth it,
because it is all leading me back home
*to myself.*

# MISPLACED

every corner of your heart you so strategically misplaced
every frozen piece you've come to believe should never sense the
touch or gaze of another every unhealed bone and every inch
you've bashed or dismissed

… all now finding their way back home,
basking in love and tenderness,
where all that deeply hides inside you,
rests in me too.

# SWEET NIGHT(S)

And on sweet, silent nights like these,
as I lay on my balcony and gaze at the stars,
I think of the love I've had, not the love I've lost.

# LOVERS OF FREEDOM

I am the ocean.
Full of surprises, depths, and secrets.
An ocean so mysterious it seems like it can't ever be fully explored.

Sometimes I silently wish I could gather the courage
to dive deeper than I ever have before
and uncover a whole new galaxy.
A forgotten world.
I imagine it's engulfed in colors
of unconditional love and freedom.

One day I will uncover all of my depths.
I will find the last forgotten pieces of my heart
and reach out to the hands of those who are still drowning.

## PURITY

I don't expect the entire world to understand.
I know the majority most likely won't, but that's okay.

I know there are many hearts, walking through this world who
won't let our cultural insecurities put out their authentic fire and
drain their waves of vast freedom.
Who will rise again and again when the world can't dare to
understand their depths.

In those, I've found my home and now I know my heart won't
ever sing alone.

## MAMA'S WORDS

Darling, can't you see?
It is your own love
you've been longing for
all along.

ON MY WAY


With my left hand holding my right
I am flowing with the current of my soul.
Through my nightmares, my wildest dreams and everything in
between I am finding my way back to who I was always meant to be.
The polarity between night and day.
The power of the sun and the depth of the moon
with energy like the ocean,
flowing back and forth,
while beaming through the darkness
and letting love
lead the way.

# CAN YOU SEE HER?

Last night I spoke with the ocean.
She's like me in some ways.
She's like all of us women.
She holds space for life and for depths words or looks could
never touch.
She lovingly holds us, moves with us and through us.
She patiently listens when tears replace words
and when storms get too dark or too heavy to bear
she continues to flow with us.
Like a mother, a daughter or a sister,
she knows love and care better than the moon knows the sun.
But we forget sometimes that even she breaks and falls apart.
Even she crawls for love sometimes
and in a world full of chaos she has no place to turn to other than
the corners of your heart,
patiently hoping you will see her too.

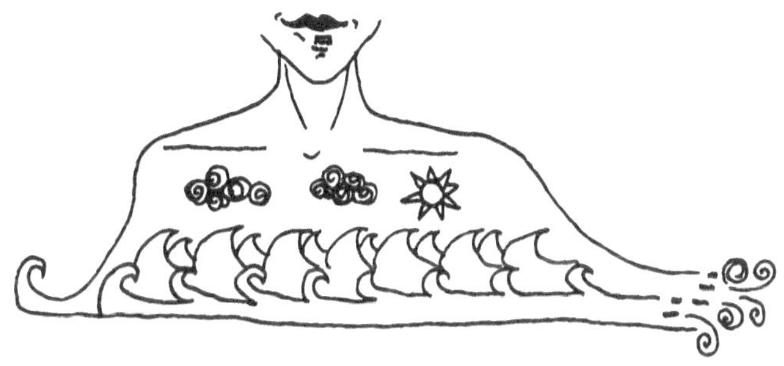

# LJUBEZEN

It's in every corner of my smile,
It's tangled up in my brain,
and it feels most at home as it peacefully rests in my heart.

Love even found its way into the darkest, most hidden parts of
myself, where now wildflowers accompany the broken pieces.

*"Welcome home"* my soul quietly whispers,
as love kisses my cheek and tenderly touches
the last broken piece of my heart.

# I SEE IT, DO YOU SEE IT TOO?


I see flowers growing from your heart
I see them peeking through the darkness
I sense them searching for your love
I hope you can soon see them too

*Thank you* for seeing me for all that I am.

# INDEX

*part 3 - full like the moon*

# ABOUT THE AUTHOR

Nika Erčulj is a writer, wellness teacher, and a trauma healing practitioner.

Her passion for sharing the vulnerable depths that most of us avoid started at a young age of fourteen, when she experienced a mental breakdown, leading her to a path of radical honesty and deep exploration.

Nika has honestly shared her battle with mental health, the ups and downs of recovery, and the joys that self-love healing can bring, inspiring thousands of individuals to find their voice, discover radical self-compassion and create their own authentic path in this world.

She has spoken on many panels, sharing her knowledge and raising awareness of mental and emotional health.

Nika continues to share her experience and knowledge with her community online. She passionately and creatively shares pieces of her heart and teaches new ways we can heal our wounds and love all parts of who we are.

Follow her journey: *@nikaerculj*

Illustrations: Kaja Judež
Design: Tea Horvat

www.ingramcontent.com/pod-product-compliance
Lightning Source LLC
Chambersburg PA
CBHW031133130726
47988CB00006B/2352